No Greater Love

MELISSA DAY

ISBN 978-1-64079-183-1 (Paperback)
ISBN 978-1-64079-184-8 (Digital)

Copyright © 2017 by Melissa Day

All rights reserved. No part of this publication may be reproduced, distributed, or transmitted in any form or by any means, including photocopying, recording, or other electronic or mechanical methods without the prior written permission of the publisher. For permission requests, solicit the publisher via the address below.

Christian Faith Publishing, Inc.
296 Chestnut Street
Meadville, PA 16335
www.christianfaithpublishing.com

Printed in the United States of America

CHAPTER 1

The Start of a Journey

I GREW UP IN THE church environment. Both of my parents were Christians. We would go to church every single Sunday. Going to church was just something that was a part of our lives. I have no clue what life would be like without church, because I've never had to live that life.

The church I grew up in was on the opposite side of the county from where my family lived. In some ways it was fun going to a church on the opposite side of the county. It allowed me to expand my "friend circle." I had two different groups of friends, my church friends and my school friends.

In other ways, it was difficult. All of my friends from church saw each other at school. They all went to the same school. I only saw them on the weekends and if we had a special event in the evenings. I sometimes felt left out or like I was behind when we saw each other on Sundays. My church friends were able to catch up with one another during the week. They were able to talk about who did what at school that week, who won the big game, whose dating who, you know … typical high school gossip. I had no clue what they were talking about most of the time.

I had other friends at school I would see throughout the week. That's where I would get my gossip from, school. We never talked much about the Lord. I was shy and didn't talk much growing up.

My parents might tell you otherwise. I didn't know if my friends went to church or not, and I certainly wasn't going to bring it up. I went my whole childhood in school not talking about Jesus.

When I was in the eleventh grade, my best friend invited me to go to a Christian club at school. I agreed to go with her. I trusted her, and I knew it had to be good if she was inviting me to go. When I arrived to the room where the club was meeting, I learned that all of my closest friends were there too. Not only were they there, they were also Christians. I still remember that day very clearly. That was the day that started my life changing experience. Apparently my friends had also been meeting at my best friend's house frequently for a Bible study, and I had no clue.

Fast forward to the summer … The summer between my junior and senior year in high school I was hanging out with my two closest friends from school. The same girl that had invited me to the Christian club and another one of our really close friends. While we were hanging out, we all three got a phone call. The timing was really funny to me. We all got a phone call within moments of each other.

The Rowan County Coordinator of Youth Commission International, the Christian club we had been attending, had called us. She expressed that she had heard about the three of us and wanted to know if we would be the student leaders for Youth Commission International at our school next year. I wasn't surprised that my friends got called, but honestly I was shocked that she would call me. My two friends that got the same phone call deserved it way more than I did. They were out going, they were involved, they were popular, and they definitely were walking a closer walk with God than I was. I was just this quiet no body that kept to myself. How was I supposed to lead a group of students into the things God had for them when I wasn't even walking closely with the Lord? I knew Jesus, I went to church, but he certainly wasn't my number one priority. I didn't deserve this honor. It didn't take me long to realize that wasn't how God or my friends saw me. This was just the beginning of the plans God had for me.

Later on that summer I had a meeting with the Rowan County Director of Youth Commission International, my two best friends and our three (yes, I said three) Campus Pastors. One of the Campus Pastors later became one of the biggest influences in my life.

One of my friends jokingly said, "We should all go around and say one fact about ourselves." Everyone thought that was a great idea, so that is exactly what we did. I said the same thing I always say when I meet someone, "I play the drums." One of our Campus Pastors said, "Really? Because I'm looking for someone to play the drums in my youth band." That following week, we met and played music together at his church for the first time.

I am a firm believer in God aligning everything perfectly to fit his plan. It turned out the new Campus Pastor of my high school's Christian club was the Youth Pastor at the same church I attended for after school care and summer camp from the time I was five years old until I turned twelve years old. Actually, that was the same exact church where I gave my life to the Lord at eight years old.

While we were hanging out at the church he told me "the kids at his church knew who God is, but they don't really know that you should live for him every day." I was shocked by that statement. How could someone not know that you should live for God every day? The more I pondered on that statement, the more I realized I had been like those kids. Even in that moment, I wasn't living for Christ every day. Instead, I was deep in sin. I had a foul mouth, I had a bad attitude, I had been disobeying my parents, and the list could go on. My eyes were opened that day, and I knew I needed to change. God was calling on me, and I needed to get my act together.

From then on out I started spending a lot of time with my new mentor, his wife, and their youth group. The more I spent time with them, the more I realized he was right. The kids were a great group of kids. They loved their families, they loved each other, and they even loved God, but they were still missing something. They were missing the relationship aspect of being a Christian.

When you have a relationship with someone, you don't just talk to them when it's convenient. You don't just see them on Sundays or think about them on holidays. You think about them all the time. That's how our relationship with Jesus should be. We should want to think about him and talk to him all the time.

I knew that was my mentor's heart for the kids. He wanted them to have a relationship with Jesus that was so close that Jesus was who they thought about all the time. It wasn't long after spending time with the Campus Pastor that I started to have the same desire in my heart.

God had been so good to me. I wanted to share all that God had done for me. I didn't want to keep it a secret any more. I wanted to talk to youth and tell them it was okay to say the name of Jesus. And most importantly, I wanted everyone to know the importance of making Jesus apart of your entire life. Jesus is my best friend, and I wanted others to make Jesus their best friend. And that was the start of my journey.

CHAPTER 2

Answering the Call

Has someone ever tried telling you something, and it didn't actually click until about the third or fourth time you heard it? I wish I could say that's never happened to me, but that wouldn't be true. In fact, it happens far too often.

Sometimes when God is trying to tell me something, I don't give him my full attention. I either ignore what he is trying to say because I don't like what I'm hearing, or I simply just don't listen to him. Let me go ahead and tell you not to learn from me in those instances. Instead, learn from my mistakes. I wish I would have given God my whole devoted attention. My life probably would have been much easier had I just listened.

When I was senior in high school, I was starting to make some big decisions in my life. Before that time, the biggest decisions I ever had to make was the sports I was going to play and the clothes I would wear that day. As a teenager, those can be some major decisions, right?

If you've ever been in high school, you know your senior year is one of the most crucial years of your life. If you're not in high school yet, you will figure it out when you get there. High school is where you start to figure out what you want to do with the rest of your life. Or if you're like me, you still don't have it all figured out years later.

It is during your junior and senior year of high school that you decide where you're going to college. If you're not going to college, where are you going to work? Are you going to enlist in the military? Those are all questions many high schoolers face every day. Knowing the answers to those questions will probably change their lives one way or another.

When I was a senior in high school, I had a dream of being an optometrist. I even did my senior project on optometry. Little did I know, God had other plans for my life. It was during my senior year that my whole life was changed forever.

Life was good. I had everything going for me. I had a lot of friends, I was the drumline captain for my high school marching band, and I was playing drums for the youth band. I thought I had everything figured out. Truth is, I didn't have everything figured out.

In September of 2009 my life was changed forever. God had already been speaking to me, but I chose to ignore him. I knew God was calling me to the ministry, but I was afraid. Because I was so afraid to go into the ministry, I chose to ignore God instead. And believe it or not, I actually told God, "No." I am sure I am the only one that has ever told God "no" before. Looking back now, it breaks my heart to know that I actually told God "no." I didn't know what going in to the ministry would look like, and it made me nervous. I wanted to stay where I was because I was comfortable.

In September of 2009, I was at our youth meeting. I still remember that night very clearly. When worship was over, I took my seat next to my best friend like I always did. My mentor was teaching that night. He spoke on Isaiah 6. Actually, I grew to love the book of Isaiah after this night. Isaiah 6:8 says, "Then I heard the voice of the Lord saying, whom shall I send? And who will go for us? And I said, here I am! Send me!"

The speaker told us that God was calling us all to something. Were we going to go where God was calling us too? After hearing him teach on Isaiah 6, I started thinking more about where God was calling me. I remembered that desire God had planted in my heart that made me want to tell everyone else about Jesus.

Unfortunately I was stubborn, so I did nothing about my call to the ministry. I remember telling my best friend that I felt like God was calling me to the ministry, but I was afraid. She told me she was proud of me and encouraged me to trust God. She was the first person, and at this point the only person, I told I felt like God was calling me to the ministry.

A few weeks later, I was at a youth rally at another church. One of my mentor's really close friends was the Youth Pastor there, and he had invited us to come to worship. We both attended worship that evening. That evening, the Youth Pastor spoke on Isaiah 6 without knowing Duane had just preached on the same thing weeks prior.

For the first time in my life, I felt something different. I felt a burning sensation in my heart. I knew God was speaking to me. I remember God calling me out and saying, "Melissa, will you go?" It was on that day in October that my answer was finally, "Yes!"

When the Youth Pastor got done speaking and the music was playing, I walked up to the front. Shaking, I got on my knees and prayed like never before. I told God to use me. I was ready!

That's not the end. You see that was a very emotional day for me. I knew I had been avoiding God's call, and my heart was finally soft. I held back a lot of tears during the service. As soon as the service was over, I got in my car and drove to the local park that was just a few minutes from my house. I was going through a trial not many people knew about. I had remembered taking long walks back there with my friends. We would go back there because it was peaceful and we would talk about everything, mostly about God. Usually, no one would be back there when we were there and we would just sit around and talk. I knew the chances of no one being back there on that day was pretty good and I was right.

I wanted to be alone with Lord, and it was the only place I could think of to go. I got out of my car and started running toward the trail. Looking back, I would never encourage a seventeen-year-old girl to go on a trail by herself. It probably wasn't the smartest thing to do, but I had one thing on my mind and that was Jesus. As soon as I got deep into the trail, I fell to me knees and cried before the Lord.

Matthew 6:6 says, "But when you pray, go into your room, close the door and pray to your Father, who is unseen. Then your Father, who sees what is done in secret, will reward you." I remember pouring my heart out before the Lord through prayer that day. It was the best feeling I had ever felt. Ever since that day, my life has been different. No matter what happened, God was there leading me down the path he had for me. Life wasn't always easy, but I know God was always there with me.

CHAPTER 3

You Are Not Alone

LONELINESS CAN BE A TERRIBLE thing. When someone is alone, bad things can happen. If you're like me, you probably think too much when you're alone. God doesn't want us to be alone. Genesis 2:18 says, "Then the Lord God said, it is not good that the man should be alone, I will make him a helper for him," and then he created Eve. God doesn't want us to be alone.

When I was in high school, a kid I knew from my youth group committed suicide. Why? Because he felt alone. Suicide is something that unfortunately happens far too often, and most of the time it's because the victim felt alone. If you don't learn anything else from this book, know you are not alone! There is a God that loves you. Deuteronomy 31:6 says, "Be strong and courageous. Do not fear or be in dread of them, for it is the Lord your God who goes with you. He will not leave you or forsake you."

When I was in my second year of college, a close friend of mine and someone I really looked up too shared a word with me. I still remember that night today. I remember where we were and what she said to me. My friend said, "Melissa, there will be a time in your life where you feel alone and forgotten, but you aren't alone. God is always with you." At the time, neither one of us realized what all I would be walking through later.

There has been a time in my life, fairly recently actually, where I also felt alone. I'm not just saying these things for fun. I really had to wrestle with loneliness. I had to make a decision to not believe the lies. The lonely feeling you have is bad news. It really can take a toll on you.

When you're like me and a lot of your friends move away and you're trying to make new friends. Or you're trying to figure out where you are called to be. When everyone around you has busy lives and you don't see your friends as often as you used too. Maybe you once found your identity in a sports team, with your job or a certain relationship. Suddenly all of that is gone, and you are once again trying to figure out who you are.

You might feel forgotten or lost. It's easy to feel forgotten when it seems as if the world is taking off and leaving you. Classmates are chasing their careers, friends are starting families. And with all of this it seems like everyone is one or two steps ahead of you. What about me? Did God forget me? I promise, God has not forgotten you.

Have you ever thought, maybe God has even bigger plans for you? He just hasn't gotten to you yet. God didn't forget you. Through everything, please know that God is there with you, he loves you, and you are not alone. Philippians 4:19 says, "And my God will supply every need of yours according to his riches in glory in Christ Jesus." The same God you see supplying all of the needs of all of the people around you is supplying your needs too. Just be patient.

One of my best friends once said, "Melissa, you cannot find your satisfaction through our friendship. I will never be able to satisfy all of your needs. Only God can satisfy your needs. When everyone else is gone, God will still be there with you." She is absolutely right. There is no one that will ever be able to satisfy all of my needs like God can. We are all humans. We are going to make mistakes. Even when man fails us, God will still be there. Even when those friendships slowly drift away because life happens, we still have our best friend, Jesus.

Matthew 28:20 says, "And behold, I am with you always, to the end of the age." God is there with us through every part of our lives, the good and the bad. Jesus says, "I will never leave nor forsake you."

If you feel alone and if you are willing, I want you to stop and pray. I want you to pray this simple prayer, or whatever God lays on your heart.

Dear Jesus,
    I know you have great plans for me. I know you love me. I renounce the lie that I am alone. I know you are here with me. Satan cannot have my joy, he cannot have my family or my friends. My joy comes from the Lord.
In Jesus's name,
Amen.

CHAPTER 4

Unshaken

HAVE YOU EVER HAD SOMETHING or someone you really cherish gone just in the blink of an eye? Everything in your life is going great. You have everything you could ever want. Maybe you have that dream job, you're the most popular kid in school. Maybe you're a star athlete or you're in a relationship with that girl or boy you've always had a crush on. Things all seem like they are really going well and then just like that those things are gone.

You go to work and find out you are being laid off. Your coach decides to cut you from the football team because you just aren't performing like you used too. Your boyfriend just broke up with you. Or maybe an accident happened that completely changed your life.

When I was fourteen years old, I was at the lake with my family. When you are fourteen years old in the state of North Carolina, you can take a boating class and earn your boating license in order to drive boats and jet skis by yourself.

I had just earned my boating license, and my dad had just bought a brand new jet ski. My parents had given me permission to drive the jet ski, while my brother tubed behind it. He was the first person I had ever pulled on the tube.

When I was driving the jet ski I went way too fast and threw my brother off the tube. We had both flipped off the tube before, but this time was different because I had been driving recklessly. My brother landed on his back and was in a lot of pain. That was basically the end of our lake trip that day.

Several days later, my brother had still been complaining about his back hurting so my parents took him to the hospital to get checked out. It was that day that my brother had been diagnosed with scoliosis. In that moment my family's whole life changed. My brother had his first of ten back surgeries at the age of thirteen.

Our lives were certainly shaken at that point. We didn't know what was going to come, but we knew our lives would never be the same. At that point everything seemed hopeless. Complications from the surgery kept coming up causing my brother to have nine more surgeries. Holidays were being spent in the hospital. Medical bills kept reaching the maximum.

It was easy for me to be mad at myself. It was easy to blame myself. Why did I have to be so rough on him? Why was I determined to flip him off the tube? Why couldn't it be me with scoliosis? Why did it have to be my little brother?

It was also easy to get mad at God. Why him? Why did this have to happen to someone as innocent and loving as my brother? He never hurt anyone; he loved everyone. He didn't deserve this. When things are shaken, it is easy to lose sight of God. It is easy to praise God when things are going well. What about when you get thrown a curve ball? It says in Romans 8:28, "And we know that for those who love God all things work together for good, for those who are called according to his purpose."

I know that God is going to one day heal my brother. I will not give up, I will continue asking. My brother has so much faith. Even when everyone else was having a hard time with the situation, he had so much faith. Right before he was taken back for his last surgery, my brother looked at his doctor and said, "Let's hurry up and get this over with. I have things to do." Even when our family was shaken, God still remained faithful and was there with us the whole time.

In January of 2016, God put a single word on my heart, "shaken." After God put that word on my heart, he asked me a question. He said, "Melissa, I'm going to shake things up, where will you stand?" My response was, "I don't know, God. I don't know where I will stand. I hope it's with you." It's easy to praise God when things are going great. It's when things start getting difficult when we're really being tested.

Things were going great for me. It was a new year, I was happy, I had a great job, I was doing ministry, and I had a great group of friends. What could possibly go wrong? I honestly didn't know why God would shake things up, but I believed he would do it.

A few days later, I was in a vehicle accident on my way to work. I was driving to work going about thirty-five miles per hour as my brakes failed. The car in front of me was stopped, and I couldn't get my car to stop in time. My car was totaled that day. This was just the beginning of my life being "shaken." I never realized how much I took for granted, especially having a vehicle, until I didn't have one. I was working a full time job and doing youth ministry at the time. I had to rely on my friends and family a lot for rides. That in itself was difficult. I hated asking people for help, but I had no choice.

On January twenty-seventh of that year I bought my first truck. I had always wanted a truck but could never afford it. I loved my new to me truck so much because I knew it was a gift from God. The night after I bought my truck, I went to my parent's house to show it off. My mom had already seen it, but my dad had not seen it, and I wanted to show him.

At the time, my grandma was living with my parents. I noticed she didn't seem like she was feeling very well. I asked my mom if she was okay just for my mom to tell me that my grandma had been getting sick a lot lately. I had no clue that would be the last time I saw her.

That weekend I had to go to Charlotte, North Carolina for my graduate school classes. As I was driving home from school, I called my mom to see if she still wanted to go to church with me in the morning. My parents had just moved to the North Carolina Mountains weeks prior, and they were in the process of looking for a church to attend. She told me she didn't think this weekend was going to work out. I immediately began to question her response. I knew something was wrong, but she wouldn't answer me. My mom told me to call her when I got home.

Curious as to what was going on, I called my mom as soon as I got home. She told me my grandma had passed away earlier that day. She had told everyone not to tell me because she knew I would be driving home alone late that night. I was close to my grandma, and she knew it was going to be hard on me to hear that kind of news. I didn't really know what to feel. In fact, I didn't feel anything. I was numb. I was shaken.

Even when you know someone you love isn't going to be with you forever, and even if you try to prepare yourself, you really are never prepared. My life was shaken, my year was shaken, and it was only January.

I wish I could say it got easier from there, but it didn't. I started to question more and more where God had called me to be. I started to wonder who it was that God had called me to be. I let go of the things distracting me from God. I distanced myself from relationships that were coming in between me and the Lord. And I started becoming more of who God had called me to be.

One of my favorite verses in the Bible is Romans 8:28, "And we know that for those who love God all things work together for good, for those who are called according to his purpose." Sometimes when God "shakes" things up he's actually got another plan in mind.

Maybe God wants to get your attention. Maybe he wants to push you harder because he knows you can handle it, and he wants you to grow even more. Maybe it's not even for you, you are just the tool. Maybe it's for someone else who might need their eyes opened to the Mighty God we serve. There were several people in the Bible whose lives were "shaken" for the greater good. When I think of someone's life being "shaken" the first person I think of is Mary.

Mary was engaged to be married to a man, named Joseph, when an angel, named Gabriel, spoke to her in a dream and said she would become pregnant. At first, Mary didn't see how it was possible since she was a virgin.

Could you imagine what it would be like to be in Mary's shoes? Could you imagine all of the scares she would face? In those days, if you had a child out of wedlock they would stone you. And what would her finance think? Would he believe she is still a virgin? Gabriel, the angel, had also said something about her son being the Son of God. He was supposed to be a king. How in the world do you raise a king?

When the day came for Mary to conceive the baby, she praised God! Mary loved God, and she trusted him. That baby boy that Mary gave birth too changed millions of lives. He made a lasting impact on this world. All because God chose Mary to give birth to his Son. Mary's life was shaken, but the outcome was amazing.

When your life gets shaken where will you stand? As it says in Matthew 7:24-27, "Everyone then who hears these words of mine and does them will be like a wise man who built his house on the rock. And the rain fell, and the floods came, and the winds blew and beat on that house, but it did not fall, because it had been founded on the rock. And everyone who does not do them will be like a foolish man who built his house on the sand. And the rain fell, and the floods came, and the winds blew and beat against that house, and it fell, and great was the fall of it."

Will you be like the wise builders who built their house on the rock? Or will you be like the foolish builders who built their house on the sand? Psalm 18:2 says, "The Lord is my rock and my fortress and my deliver, my God, my rock, in whom I take refuge, my shield, and the horn of my salvation, my stronghold." Jesus is the rock. When you are standing on Jesus you are standing on the rock, and you will not be shaken.

Sometimes God shakes things up so that his glory can be revealed. One of my favorite passages from the Bible is in the book of John. There was a man born blind. As Jesus walked passed him, his disciples asked him, "Rabbi, who sinned? This man or his parents that he was born blind?" Jesus answered, "It is not this man that sinned, or his parents, that he was born blind, but that the works of God might be displayed in him."

That day, Jesus healed this man. When he was healed no one recognized him. When the man told others that this man, Jesus, healed him, they refused to believe him. His neighbors didn't recognized him, his parents disowned him, and he was kicked out of his community. I can imagine his life was pretty shaken.

When Jesus heard that he had been cast out from his community, he went and found him. Jesus asked the man if he believed in the Son of Man. The man replied, "Who is he, sir? That I may believe in him." Jesus said to him, "You have seen him, and it is he who is speaking to you." The man said "Lord, I believe," and he worshiped him. That day, the man that has just lost all of his family and his "friends" gained the best friend you could ever have. God took that shaken moment and turned it into something beautiful. When things get "shaken" turn to God, stand with God, and you will not be shaken.

CHAPTER 5

A Friend Loves at All Times

EVERYONE HAS PROBABLY HAD AT least one friend in their lifetime. From the time we are first born, we start making friends. I've learned in the short life I've lived that the best people at making friends are children. They don't really know the word "hate." At least, in my experience they haven't really known or understood the word "hate." That's something we teach them, whether we realize it or not.

So what makes a good friend? Someone that's always there. Someone you can talk to. Someone you have fun with. Those are all answers you might here. You might have other responses as to what makes a good friend. The first friend I ever remember having became my friend when we were only two years old. We're still friends today. Not many people can say they are blessed to have the same best friends for twenty plus years, but God has really blessed my family in that sense. Our parents are best friends, our brothers are best friends. Life without those friends is just unimaginable for our families.

So what makes them "best friends?" To me, a best friend is someone you can have fun with, but someone you can be real with as well. They know you inside and out. They love you, care for you, and protect you. Most importantly, they encourage you, build you up, and point you to God. If you ask why they are our best friends, that's why. No matter what, they have always been encouraging and great examples of the way to live your life fully for God. You can be that type of friend for people too. Even if you haven't known someone for twenty plus years, you can still be a good friend, maybe even a "best friend" to them. My best friends are the ones that have always pointed me to the Lord.

Sure, we've had our moments. Trust me, being best friends with someone since you were two years old is hard. There's been times where we've argued, maybe said things we didn't mean, but at the end of the day we were still friends. The Bible tells us that "a friend loves at all times." No matter what the circumstance is, they still love you and you love them. That's a friend.

I will be the first to tell you I have not always been a good friend to others. There have been times when I've thought about myself before someone else, someone else that I really cared a lot about. There were times when I got jealous of my friends or I said things that weren't nice. We're human. It's going to happen, but that doesn't happen with God. Did you know that Jesus calls you a friend?

John 15:15 says, "No longer do I call you servants, for the servant does not know what his master is doing; but I have called you friends, for all that I have heard from my Father I have made known to you." Jesus has called you a friend, because he loves you. He wants to have a relationship with you.

Previously I mentioned how I've known my best friend since I was two years old. When you've known someone like that you're whole life, sometimes they feel closer to you than a best friend. He's like a brother to me. Actually I call his parents "Mom and Dad" and growing up in school together, everyone thought we were related. We started telling people we were related because we were tired of them asking, and it seemed like we were. I went to his family reunions, his family spent every weekend at our house. If they weren't at our house, you could almost guarantee we were at their house. He was and is a brother.

God says, "There is a friend that sticks closer than a brother." So if he's my best friend and like a brother, is it really possible for there to be a friend that is closer than a brother? Yes! The answer is yes! There is a friend that sticks closer than a brother. It's Jesus.

If you ask me the two most important things you can have in a friendship, it's listening and unconditional love. It wasn't always that way for me. Recently, I really had to learn to value what my friends said. You see, there was a friend I called a best friend. We were really close, but I damaged our friendship. Why? Because I didn't value the words she said. I didn't listen to her. She knew I didn't care what she had to say, and she started distancing herself from me. I didn't see it, I was blind. I was so caught up in myself, I started putting myself before her. When it was too late and she was gone, I began to ask God why. Why would that friend all of a sudden not want anything to do with me?

God spoke right to my heart. I still remember that day very clearly. I remember God saying, "Melissa, you're not valuing what she's saying. You're not listening to her. You're thinking about yourself more than you're thinking about your friend. That's not a friendship." Talking about a punch right to the heart! Can you imagine God saying something like that to you? Has he said something like that to you before? It's tough.

That night, I immediately fell to my knees and cried out to God. "God, change me, change my heart! I want to be a friend like you to others." I am so blessed because God heard my prayer, he opened my eyes, he changed my heart, and he redeemed my friendship.

Let me tell you, if there is anyone who can teach you how to be a good friend it's God. John 15:13 says, "Greater love has no one than this, that someone lay down his life for his friends." That is love, that is friendship! Jesus did that. He did it for all of us. Jesus still lays down his life for me every single day. When I make mistakes, who is always there to pick me up? Who always forgives me? Who is always there for me to talk to? Who has seen me at my worst and at my best? Jesus! Jesus laid down his life for us, when he died on the cross.

Just like Jesus laid down his life for us, we can lay down our lives for our friends. How do we lay down our lives for our friends? We listen to them and pray for them. We simply smile when we pass by them. That might be the only smile they get that day. If our friends are sitting alone in the cafeteria, we can sit with them. There are so many ways we can lay down our lives for our friends. I know God will show you other ways to lay down your life, if you ask him. Look for ways to be a good friend, God will show you. It's not a burden to lay down your life, it's a joy! And you will be blessed by it.

CHAPTER 6

Learning to Wait

PATIENCE IS SOMETHING I HAVE always struggled with. I am not a patient person. Growing up, my parents taught me how to earn, spend, and save money. I was really good at earning and spending money, but not very good at saving it. When I saw something I wanted, I would buy it. My parents tried saying things like, "Melissa, your birthday is coming up. Why don't you wait until you see what you get for your birthday?" or "Christmas is right around the corner. Wait and see if you get it for Christmas." Did I have a hard time with that? Yes. I had a hard time being patient. I didn't want to wait. I wanted it then.

Over the past couple of years, I believe God has really been speaking to me about patience and teaching me to be patient. It's not something that comes natural for me, that's for sure. Being patient can certainly be a good thing.

Isaiah 40:31 says, "But they who wait for the Lord shall renew their strength; they shall mount up with wings like eagles; they shall run and not be weary; they shall walk and not faint." God has good things when you wait for him. Sometimes it's hard to wait on God. I know for me, it was. Sometimes when we come across that new toy we've always wanted, we're looking for a job or even searching for that perfect car, it's hard to wait.

When I was sixteen years old, I started the process of "car searching" with my parents. I had always wanted a truck, but a truck wasn't what I was going to get. My parents had told me they were going to buy my first car. I had asked them about getting a truck but they explained to me how they wanted me to have a smaller car while I was learning how to drive, and the gas for a truck would be too expensive. At first, I was sad that I wouldn't be getting a truck, but I was very thankful for everything my parents were doing for me. They bought me a brand new Toyota Yaris, and I loved it so much. It was mine, and my parents got it for me, therefore it was special to me.

When I was twenty-three years old, I was in an automobile accident that totaled my car. I was left having to find a new vehicle. I still had it in the back of my mind that I had always wanted a truck. I had looked in to trucks, but none of them were in my price range at the time. Eventually, I stopped looking online and went to a dealership to ask them what they had to offer. I had never bought a vehicle on my own before, so everything was a learning process to me. When I told them what I wanted and my price range, they said, "Well, you won't find that here, or possibly anywhere." They offered to help me find another vehicle if I wanted. Disappointed, I knew I needed a vehicle as soon as possible so I agreed to go inside and chat with one of the salesman.

We looked at trucks again, but all of them were too expensive. After a little while, we decided to start looking at other vehicles. As we were flipping through the other vehicles on the website of the car dealership, the sales man's voice changed to a voice of excitement. He had found a truck online on the wrong page. Not only that, it was just two hundred dollars above my price range. The truck had been at another store, so the salesman offered to bring the truck over the next day so that I could test drive it. Seeing as I knew nothing about vehicles and what to listen for when test driving a vehicle, a friend of mine went with me to test drive the truck. I immediately fell in love with the truck, but I didn't want to get my hopes up if that wasn't the vehicle I was supposed to have.

I told the salesman I loved the vehicle but I just couldn't quite afford it at the price it was at. After the man talked for a little while to his supervisor, it was decided that they would come down on the price to meet my price range! Thrilled, I went home with the truck that night! God really blessed me in this situation. My parents were right. I didn't need a truck when I was only sixteen years old. It was way too big and too expensive for me. It was hard waiting. I had dreamed day and night about one day having a truck. When I was ready to give up, God said, "Wait! I have something even better for you." God knew I would one day be driving the vehicle of my dreams. I just had to wait until it was the right timing. I have come to realize that our timing is so different than God's timing, but God's timing is perfect. I love my truck because I know it is a gift from God.

Waiting can be tough, but it is so worth it. Psalm 27:14 says, "Wait for the Lord; be strong, and let your heart take courage; wait for the Lord!" God has good things for you if you just wait on him.

As it says in Psalm 37:4-5, "Delight yourself in the Lord, and he will give you the desires of your heart. Commit your way to the Lord; trust in him and he will act." God knows the desires of your heart. He knows what you need and what you want. Just trust in him. He wants good things for you, and he will give you good things, you just have to trust him. God knows what's best for us. He's not going to give us something that might in turn be harmful to us. He only wants to give us good things.

So whatever it is you're wanting, trust God. Whether it's a new car, a new job. Maybe it's a new house, a spouse or even a child. Maybe it's none of those things. Maybe you long for a past friendship to be restored. Maybe you've been praying that your mom or your dad would become Christians, and you're starting to lose hope, hope in God, hope in yourself, hope in your parents. Don't give up, keep trusting God. Lay all of those things at the feet of God.

I once had a friend of mine tell me to give it all to the Lord. As someone that wants to be in control, it's hard laying everything down before the Lord, but it's so worth it. I had the privilege of laying everything down before God a few times recently. I got to lay down all of my desires. I got to lay down my family, my friendships, my career, and even all of my dreams. It wasn't a burden. It was a joy! When I laid those things down, it was as if a huge weight was lifted off my shoulders. I got to trust God with my entire life. I got to lay it all before him and let him do what he wanted with my life.

Since then, my life has been completely different. I have the best job I've ever had, my family has grown closer together, my friendships are different, and I am living my dream. God knew what was best for me, and he made a way. It's okay to lay down those things more than once. I know I had too. I want to encourage you, don't give up! Keep laying them down and keep trusting God. I can assure you, you will see fruit from it. Just keep waiting on the Lord, and he will give you good things!

CHAPTER 7

Giving It All

As an athlete and musician, I learned the term "giving it all" at a very young age. I believe we are all born with motivation but then we choose to let go of it and become lazy as we get older. From the time I could walk, I always enjoyed playing basketball. It was one of my favorite sports. Every day after school I would shoot basketball with a group of friends. As we got older, all of those friends grew to be much taller than me. I didn't let that stop me, I just knew I would have to work harder. I started focusing on other areas that could come to my advantage like my speed and my ball handling skills. I loved basketball, and I didn't want my height to be something that got in the way.

When I was in middle school my coach taught us to give it our all. He pushed us until we couldn't go anymore. I appreciate him pushing us so hard because it taught me so much about doing well in all that I do. Every day during practice, we would have to run sprints. When you're on the last leg of your sprint and you're tired, what do you do? You speed up, you push through, and you give it everything you have until the very end. That's giving your all.

In the same way, we can give it our all in our spiritual journey. Why wouldn't we give it all? Jesus gave it all for us when he gave up his life for us. Hebrews 12:1-2 says, "Therefore, since we are surrounded by so great a cloud of witnesses, let us also lay aside every weight, and sin which clings so closely, and let us run with endurance the race that is set before us, looking to Jesus, the founder and perfecter of our faith, who for the joy that was set before him endured the cross, despising the shame, and is seated at the right hand of the throne of God."

In a time where our world is getting scarier by the day, we can't back down. Run the race as if you are the only one that can win. Giving it all is simple, just live a life that would be pleasing to God. How do you "give it all" in your walk with God? Here's my thoughts on some ways to give it all.

Spend time with God. This is the most important thing you can do. Spend time reading his word, worshiping him, and of course talking to him in prayer. You would be surprised how much your life changes just by spending time with God. Even if you're just saying simple prayers throughout the day, at least you're thinking about God. God loves for us to spend time with him. Sometimes we get so caught up in our busy lives that we forget about God, I know I have, but it doesn't have to be like that anymore. My favorite time to talk with God is when I'm driving to work in the mornings. What else can you do during that time by yourself? It's easy to do.

Another way to run the race is by building each other up. 1 Thessalonians 5:11 says, "Therefore encourage one another and build one another up, just as you are doing." No one likes someone who is demeaning them all the time. Build each other up, encourage one another. When someone encourages me in the things I'm doing, it gives me strength. It makes me feel like I'm doing something with a purpose. Everyone needs to be encouraged from time to time, so don't be afraid to let the encouraging words flow.

The last way to run the race is to lay down your life. No, it's not quite as scary as it seems. John 15:13 says, "Greater love has no one than this, that someone lay down his life for his friends." What does it mean to lay down your life? Just that! Lay down your life! We are called to die daily. We are called to carry our cross. When we lay down our lives we are dying daily. Laying down your life simply means putting others before you. When Jesus laid down his life for us, he thought about us more than himself. No, it doesn't mean we literally have to die on a cross. However, it does mean we need to "die."

It is my prayer that we will all run the race like it's the last hundred yards. When worldly things drag us down, we can know there is a prize that is far greater than any prize worldly things can give us. The prize we're after is eternal life. Jesus died for us so that we could have eternal life, the least we can do is give him our all.

CHAPTER 8

You Are Worth It

WHILE SITTING IN ONE OF my marketing classes in college, my professor started lecturing the class on knowing our worth. He asked us if we had ever thought about our worth. Honestly, I had never thought about my worth before. It was something that never crossed my mind. The point of the lecture was to get students thinking about how much they are worth in the sense of finding a job. He wanted us to know that there would be people that try to take advantage of our worth, and he was teaching us to not sell ourselves short.

So do you know how much you are worth? It's something fun to think about. Genesis 1:27 English Standard Version says, "So God created man in his own image, in the image of God he created him; male and female he created them." That is how much you are worth! God loves you so much that he created you in his own image. Later on in Genesis 1:28, God says, "Have dominion over the fish of the sea and over the birds of the heavens and over every living thing that moves on the earth." God could have chosen anything to rule the earth, but he chose us, because he thought that highly of us.

If you ever hear "you're not worth it" or "you don't amount to anything" don't believe those lies. You are worth it! Sometimes, it's easy to fall into the trap of thinking we're not good enough. We have it in our minds that there is always going to be someone out there that is smarter, cooler, better looking or more valuable than us. The world will tell us that's true. There will always be someone smarter than us. There will be someone cooler or better looking than we are. God tells us that he loves us the same.

Matthew 10:30-31 says, "But even the hairs of your head are all numbered. Fear not, therefore; you are of more value than many sparrows." That is your worth! You are worth so much that even the hairs on your head are numbered. That means that God knows every inch of your body, and he cares about it, even something as small as a tiny piece of hair. God says, "Before I formed you in the womb I knew you" (Jeremiah 1:5). God knows you, he knows your name. You are worth it to him.

I used to compare myself to other people all the time. I didn't think I could measure up. I always thought others were going much farther than I was. I remember a time when I was in high school, where a friend of mine really spoke into my life about my worth. I was wrestling with the idea of going into the ministry full time. I was having a hard time with it. I knew God was calling me out, but I didn't think I was good enough.

When we compare ourselves to others what we're actually doing is looking for affirmation from things that aren't the Lord's. Let's be real here. If you're comparing yourself to someone else, why? Why are you comparing yourself to them? Do you want someone to notice you? Is that what you're after? That's what I was after. I was competing in a competition that didn't even make sense. I was looking for affirmation in other things that weren't the Lord's. I was looking for affirmation in my job, my relationships, and my academics instead of looking for affirmation in the Lord. When we're really looking for affirmation in the Lord, instead of earthly things, we won't worry about if we measure up or not. In God's eyes, you do measure up!

It was my senior year in high school. I was sitting on my friend's porch texting another friend. The friend I was texting was the same friend that had walked with me and stood beside me the whole time during my journey of noticing my calling. I was telling her I didn't think I would be good enough. Why me? Why little old Melissa? I couldn't even talk to my friends about Jesus without getting super nervous. How was I supposed to talk to others? I knew God was changing my life, he was training me, but I didn't understand why he would waist his time on me. There were so many other people out there, I could have named a whole list, that would have done a much better job at going in to the ministry, but God chose me. That day, I was texting my friend, telling her how I didn't understand why God would choose me. I remember sending a text message that literally said, "Why me?" Her response was, "He does pick all of the dorky ones, doesn't he? You deserve it though. You have a grand amount of faith, and all he asks for is a mustard seed size."

I'll be honest, I laughed when she sent me that text. However, seven plus years later, those words still reign true. That response would have been true had she sent me that text message two thousand years ago. Assuming we were both around then and that there was texting. God does pick all of the "dorky ones." If you think you're not worth it, look at Zacchaeus.

Zacchaeus was a tax collector in Jericho. Not only that, he was a mean man. As Jesus was passing through the town, Zacchaeus wanted to see who he was, but he couldn't because he was so small. Zacchaeus climbed in a sycamore tree to see Jesus, who was about to pass him. As Jesus passed Zacchaeus, he hollered out to him and told him to come down because he must stay at his house that day.

Jesus chose the sinner, he chose the smallest in the crowd, because he thought he was worth it. That day Zacchaeus became a follower of Christ. Just like Zacchaeus, you are worth it! You are so valuable to God that he would leave his ninety-nine sheep to go after the one that was lost. That is your value. Don't sell yourself short. God loves you so much, and you are worth it to him!

CHAPTER 9

An Open Invitation

As we head into the final chapter of this book, I don't want to stop writing before telling you that you have an open invitation. An open invitation to be in a relationship with God. I can honestly say that there is no greater love than the love that God has for you. God loves you so much that he sees passed all of your flaws and just sees you. Romans 3:23 says, "For all have sinned and fall short of the glory of God." We are all sinners. We are going to make mistakes.

Romans 6:23 says, "For the wages of sin is death, but the free gift of God is eternal life in Christ Jesus our Lord." There has to be a price we pay when we sin, and that price is death. However, we don't have to die because God gives us a free gift. He gives us eternal life. Romans 5:8 says, "While we were still sinners, Christ died for us." This is why we don't have to pay death. Christ did it for us when he died on the cross. We sinned, and Christ paid our debts.

Romans 10:13 says, "Anyone who calls on the name of the Lord will be saved." God doesn't just hand pick the people he wants to save. It says "anyone" who calls on his name will be saved. That's you and me. We are anyone! So Christ has already paid our debts just like he paid the debts of our neighbors, our friends, our teammates.

How do we call on the name of the Lord? It's simple. Romans 10:9-10 says, "But if you confess with your mouth that Jesus is Lord and believe in your heart that God raised him from the dead, you will be saved. For with the heart one believes and is justified, and with the mouth one confesses and is saved."

If you have never confessed that Jesus is Lord, God is inviting you to do so right now in this moment. Will you take the invitation? You can make God the author of your life, today, just by confessing that he is Lord. If you're looking for a best friend, someone you can always talk to, someone who loves you unconditionally, find Jesus! He is the only one that will be able to satisfy all of your needs. He is the only one that will love you unconditionally. Man will mess up. Man will fail you. Jesus will never make a mistake.

Deuteronomy 31:6 says, "Be strong and courageous. Do not fear or be in dread of them, for it is the Lord your God who goes with you. He will not leave you or forsake you." God will never leave you. He will be there with you through the fire and the storm. He will be with you on the mountain and the valley. Are you going to accept his invitation? Anyone can accept the invitation of Christ. It's an open invitation. What will you do?

About the Author

MELISSA DAY IS A YOUNG southern girl who has learned the importance of making God a part of her everyday life. Born and raised in North Carolina, she has learned to love the south and all it has to offer. Melissa is a graduate of Western Carolina University, located in the mountains of North Carolina, where she studied Communications. She loved the mountains so much she decided to make them her home shortly after graduating college. Melissa is currently working on her Masters in Divinity at Gordon-Conwell Theological Seminary. She is a practicing musician, playing drum set and guitar. Melissa also loves to write, and publishing her first book is a dream come true.

Melissa has known that she was called into the ministry since she was a senior in high school, and writing this book is just one of many ways she is trying to reach people for the good of the Kingdom. She has such a big heart for other people and will do anything to try and make you feel at home. In her free time (whenever she can find it), she likes to play and write music as well as just hang out with her family and friends.

Melissa dreams big and doesn't care where life takes her, as long as it is God's will for her life, and she knows she is following God's heart, she will go. If this book inspires or helps just one person, to Melissa, it will all be worth it. God bless.

CPSIA information can be obtained
at www.ICGtesting.com
Printed in the USA
LVOW11s0407070917
547834LV00001B/53/P